Seldom Croaked The Hawk

DANIEL MCCOSH

© 2021 Daniel McCosh

Bibliografische Information der Deutschen Nationalbibliothek:

Die Deutsche Nationalbibliothek verzeichnet diese Publikation in der Deutschen Nationalbibliografie; detaillierte bibliografische Daten sind im Internet über http://dnb.dnb.de abrufbar.

Cover and Design: Claudia Habermann & Daniel McCosh

Illustrations: p. 11, 31, 25, 43 © Claudia Habermann (http://instagram.com/c.h.design)

Page logo: © Fajar Nugroho, 123RF.com

Publisher and printing: BoD – Books on Demand, Norderstedt, Germany

Seldom Croaked The Hawk/ Daniel McCosh -- 1st ed.

ISBN 978-3-7534257-0-2

Layout ©2020 BookDesignTemplates.com

Contents

TEACHING TALES

Ever one for a grand entrance
   He swooped onto discarded branches
   Hopping from foot to foot.
   At home in the air, it might've been enquired
   How his bandy legs could bear a body
   Hewn from the blackwood bear;
   He would've rebuffed this impudence with a haughty caw.

He inclined to tell his teaching tales
   With a choice morsel beak-dangling.
   He digested reality;
   Spat it back out,
   Distaste of a scorned sommelier.

Seated on stone, he patiently drew attention
   To unfamiliar creatures who had found new life
   In the retreat of a dominant species.
   My thoughts faded into the stream as fishtails thrashed
   The water, cleansing a worrisome soul.
   He washed his face and took leave
   Circling back, homeward-bound.

SIALIA

Sialia, an idea of music.
   Mingus knew you too
   Through his patient true-blue.
   Lend me your voice
   So I may know more.

Sing me the sweetest song
   From the highest branch,
   Until my blood runs blue
   In honour of you.
   The song is the soul
   Of your existence.

Sialia, sialia, sialia.
   Whispering pines.
   Love is your chorus.
   Sialia, sialia, sialia.
   We could ascend forever.

GOLDFINCH

Tapdancing on the drainpipe,
   Watch her reel and curl.
   The heavens open
   Letting her bathwater in.
   Through her regal call
   Bill proud and stout.
   Shrill – trill –
   A colourful pout.
   Opening to speak.

Wings spread
   She brings
   Golden bolus.
   My daily medicine.
   Absolves my sin
   Not to spread my arms and sing.

Shrill – trill – a shriek.
   Sunlight kissing
   Her tender beak.
   She casts a shadow
   On my window
   Until I join in.

BIRD COLONEL

Bird colonel in the forest, whispers:
  Wald.Wiese.Wasser
  (Forest, Meadows, Water).
  He fingers mellow branches
  Gingerly grasping his lapels.

March, colonel!
  March is the month, they sing:
  Welcome spring! March, colonel!
  Raise your baton, not your gun.
  Count your soloists in: the concert begins.

Nestled in an overgrowth,
  We lend our ears to the sound.
  As the morning chorus
  Rises from all around.

ORCHIDEA

How the woodwind blows;
  Ca-ca-castanets,
  Pomp and circumstance,
  Trombone and happenstance.

Mandolin magnificence
  Joyous and free.
  Nature's chief delight, that we live
  and give freely, as heaven bestows fine music.

During the dance of a graceful couple
  The dew glides glissando on the orchid stem
  Descending dramatically onto a tambourine.
  Applause – ovations,
  And the hall falls silent again,
  With the murderous thud of bare hands on timpani.

BLESSINGS

Three blessings on the windowsill:
   Chirping trinity of hope, joy and peace,
   Humanity and nature coexist.
   From the safety of a bird's eye view
   Three messengers in their red caps bless our homes,
   Their golden feathers welcome here.

When peasant pigeons slip through the spikes
   They seem to become glistening peacocks –
   Do they really bring curses?
   Through their gawdy eye-beads
   I only see another equal creature.

DANIEL MCCOSH — SELDOM CROAKED THE HAWK

STOP, THIEF!

Reprobate! Oh, what you do not misappropriate!
    Having stolen the family's silver,
    Scattering pearls on the sill,
    You give a mischievous bow and run, quickstep.

The chief thief scarpers over the gables,
    Hoarder of secret treasures.
    His cronies keep lookout;
    The plot thickens like Kimchi.

RASPUTIN'S SECRET

When peasants and petty criminals seek to rise
   The further they later fall, from bridges.
   Rasputin was almost two metres tall.

What makes a good leader?
   Charlatans, mystics and healers?
   Or a sense of rhythm
   On steed and between sheets?
   In a film about his life
   He was played by a bear.
   Debauched and dissolute
   Mesmerizing the court.

Outside his doors
   The sick pleaded from dawn until late.
   A survivor of poisoned wine; pistol shots,
   He was finally fed to the Tura
   Where his words froze, rasping
   In dark waters.

LASHES

He wrote a hundred dreams each night
   And imprisoned them in vellum
   Until they numbered infinitely
   Of order and genus. The pages flew

To where he could see *similaria* emerge
   Beyond the obvious and all the more striking:
   Paramecia use their lashes for progress,
   Dictators use their lashes for progress,
   Evolution has not always made the best choices.

PALACE OF VARIETIES

Inside the palace of varieties,
    The burlesque and vaudevillian culture clash
    In the culture club.

Fabergé circuses, the rise
    And fall of the music halls
    Sentenced by burnt popcorn
    And reluctant reels.

The stage never ready
    For the next sex act.

A finite stream of entertainment
    Even thinner than cellulose.

DESTINATIONS

I hear solar fanfare from the horn.
  Acid raindrops polarize the dawn.
  Spear-like bodies
  Flash diamond tips: the spears, the drums, the hunt
  Chasing mechanical animals.

A race that is drawn by quarterbeat.
  Rising blue trains elevated by magnetism.
  Future echoes of a sanitized state
  Sending shockwaves in electrostatic clicks;
  Remorse code in an emergency;
  The rivers bleed quicksilver.

HEADWINDS

A marine-green marine fuses through moody, purple head-
winds
Firing splashes of rust that corrode in muddy water.
Sour acid rain stains orange chroma again
The water runs; a marbled stream to the rhythm
of a dripping tap.

Colours ebb and flow and embrace the bare metal
etched by smoky clouds of blue and crimson;
The darker the colours, the higher they fly.
Illogical smudges on string vest canvas.

BAREFOOT AT MIDNIGHT

The night sequin- shimmered as we lost ourselves.
I think he said it was *Youkali* or some kind of utopian
Sehnsucht.
Words finely curated like *Gesamtkunstwerk* or *Sprachgesang*.
Weltkultur sprouting like colonial crocus.

Paper lanterns faded at a summer garden party.
The evening passed; the big band droned dull brass.
Whilst we dreamt of escaping and dancing
Barefoot at midnight
To rhythms of our own making.
Finding soul music in the stars.

JAZZ POETS

He blew rolling notes with a healing grace
   Between the mind's ears.
   Straight to the heart.
   Rolling those bones.
   Rolling those bones.
   Straight back home.

There was church music:
   Tambourines, then Ellington
   (His father's crystal).
   Poetry born from straight connections;
   Improvised magic.

That cat is prowling, that cat is
   Howling for meaning now.
   Bouncing and rolling
   Into the city's summer night.

DANIEL MCCOSH — SELDOM CROAKED THE HAWK

SIDE A

Enter my church
   To bells that chime and flood the air with waves.
   Purple pews and daubs of royal blue.
   Remembering Hadrian's wall.
   War is in the stones; the people were ever divided,
   But our ancestors reside in our consciousness.

Now you are climbing towers in corridors.
   Bell pullers float above carpets stained with oil paints.
   Suddenly, there is a mosquito in one ear.
   Distant bells mark *time to leave this space.*

Sedate and comfortable
   As the twilight turns aubergine outside the window.
   A piano roll settles a perforated blanket of snowy calm.

Verdigris and tangerine are daintily speckled
   On the jaundiced toy piano.
   Aquarelle flows and fades.
   Each brush stroke releases a taint of camphor and
   turpentine.
   Varnish is applied;
   Reflection on the artist through a clear coat.

SIDE B

Reels spin in a post-gothic hymn,
  Rising to the buttresses, mixing purple with the grey,
  In a sweeping gesture that wakes bronze raven sculptures,
  With a portrait of sadness, etched onto magnetic tape.

From the cathedral ruins, fleeing to a cumuliform sanctuary
  Improbable architecture is suspended on a lullaby:
  The heavens open with a chorus of the purest, silver-plated
  labyrinths.
  It ends with a perfect chord, a pristine palette of rose-pinks
  and powder blues
  celebrating our birth.

DANIEL MCCOSH — SELDOM CROAKED THE HAWK

SIDE C

You make a theatrical entrance to this conversation
   Turning muddy brown brighter with each swelling chorus.

Clay and umber, your body smeared with soil.
   Forest sprawling across hills.
   We drink from rivers and bottle-green lakes.
   Speckles of dust catching in our throats
   Easily diluted by pale blue sunshine.

Reflections shimmer on the water
   Tweeters ripple and radiate sweetness.
   The shadows of branches hang slate and charcoal
   Dark green twine snares the apricots

Deep purples fill the vineyards;
   The world becomes a swollen plum.
   Dragonflies dissipate the amber moments;
   Their wings are cool on terracotta tiles.

SIDE D

Drawing to a sanguine end
  The palette of a lifelong work is expended.
  Fatigue evident in fugues of blue, grey and white
  From a bold master to an impressionistic sigh.
  The urgency of imminent departure
  Has been painted, with the peal of a silver bell
  Frozen in an arctic sunset.

A bow draws a bloody streak.
  Plasma diffuses lucidly, in oily, marble slicks
  Speckled with tawny feathers.
  A wooden puppet driven by automatons and cams
  Clinically dissects every shade of burgundy.
  Chrome eyes reflecting the soul of an artist
  Who has left you blinded in the sand.

MESSAGES IN THE SAND

Humanity has written of salvation:
  It tastes better than lead-poisoned water.
  A reminder to each and every one of you
  That we all make up the deity
  That decides our fate.

On the banks of the perfumed river
  History remembers the fragrant blossoms
  That will return again in our elevated consciousness:
  When we remember to love
  Our once imperial cities
  With their spices of every colour.

Sandstorms come from the breath of wise sages
  Blowing ashes from parched hands.
  The sand that builds glasshouses
  Where we can safely reside in a dreamscape.
  The water will return, but will we?

COAL

Coal that powers our dirtiest dreams,
   The fuel that is tearing the world apart.
   Smoke from the colliery escapes the pit.
   Miners rise above the earth with blackened faces,
   Onyx lumps have long-replaced their sclerae
   The empty stare of a life lost underground;
   The price they pay for an honest wage.

EXTRAVAGANT VENUS

Pepper says: 'If I had a plane
   Then we'd all fly to Paris'.
   I say to Pepper, 'If I had a flame
   We'd set the *Champs-Élysées* on fire'.

Wicked beauty can cause
   A bloody nose on the subway.
   Those who get home unscathed
   Are usually the young ones.

Meet me on Fifth street,
   We'll have a ball.

Octavia says:
   'I hope that the way I look
   Puts money in my pocket'.

Venus says: 'I want to get married
   In a church, in white.
   I want to be on canvas
   In a high-fashion world.'

All of these dreams
   Poster the walls of safe houses.
   Vogue makes life a dance,

Defying its hardships
   With fierce competition.

They found Venus after four days,
   Strangled under her bed,
   In a sleazy hotel room,
   While Paris was burning.

BRIGHTER

Even if tomorrow's blue dress
    Has been worn before
    Silk, sequins and glitter will never fade from vogue, as war.
    Misanthropy just needs a brighter coat
    And a thicker skin.

The stars will never fade
    So long as we are dancing, with tea-stained thighs
    That distract their Blitzkrieg hearts
    And hide our tear-stained eyes
    Make-believe gives our men something to fight for.

THREADS

In another life she wove

                    dreams

           from

              threads.

But sleeping on the pavement
  In front of the closed gallery;
  It seems that threadbare existence
  Is really no existence at all.
  Our artists deserve more.

NISHIKIGOI

In a walled garden
   Nishikigoi lie tranquil in the mirror pool.

Marble orange
   Melting into albumen.

The Tancho fins fly a sunrise flag
   In peaceful waters.

IMMORTALITY

Sunday afternoon reveala the secret of immortality

Among the corals, a *Turritopsis Dohrnii* peeps.
From its tentacle sleeves slides a victorious card.
Trumping the aces.

Returning to its juvenile polyp.
The poster child of reincarnation, dancing eternally
Flourishing, fluorescent tentacle friend:
Mostly water, but an endearing fellow
If left to its own devices.

PAINTING THE SEA

Gravel lies scattered across the causeway
  Fragmenting greens and blues from whites.
  Framed by streaked panes from a lost century
  Painted by hurried worker-man's hands.
  The clouds are rolling cyclones;
  Gulls flee in peril from the whipping spray

Caught in the jetstream.
  Mermaids chatter in melodious, silver tongues
  A muffled underwater phonograph
  Separated from the airwaves by many leagues.

Sinking with the merfolk
  Gratefully imbibing air from gracious lips.
  At greater depths, the pressure builds to a blackout
  Floating a painting silently from its whalebone frame.
  The cavernous gallery implodes with sonar clicks.

Perfect inertia leaves a vacuum of sorrowful strings.
  Wide and energetic strokes,
  Consumed by immeasurable power of water dynasties,
  submerging orchids.

Bodies jettisoned to the shore in joyous exhaustion.
  The serenity of composition *is an incredulous score.*

MERCURY

I see the sea.
  Taste the spray
  With my hair.

Running on sand.
  Running on quicksilver sand.
  Kicking up Mercury.

DANIEL MCCOSH — SELDOM CROAKED THE HAWK

YELLOW SOU'WESTER

The sound of a single teardrop on a drum
   Is the sum of all fears
   That mushroom inside us.

In the time it takes for a beat
   To pass –
   Another sou'wester
   Will weather the storm.
   The rhythm will grow stronger.

And
   The
   Beat

Will
   Go
   On.

FEATHERS IN THE SAND

I am halo.
  White espadrilles
  Kicking sand in the spume.

We live in rings
  Inside cleansing, winding coastlines.

Asymmetry is pyrtemmys tcefreP.
  Ammonites worn smooth with time
  Form eternal circles, rings, spirals in our hands.
  The shore washes the craters we leave into oblivion.

Stones woven between our fingers:
  Obsidian, jade, aquamarine.
  The perfect sea; the perfect scene
  Welcoming our human imperfection
  Wiping the slate clean –

The gulls that watch leave their memories
  As feathers in the sand.

WIND SPIRITS

At night, I open the windows to let the wind spirits in.
 The cornstalks crackle; pale tallow in the moonlight.
 The howling gales swirl; an endless sea of fricatives in my
 head.
 Surging waves are broken into snares of change, choice and
 church.
 Messages on parchment, in silver script.
 Brother crow is scratching impatiently at the windowpane
 of the crypt.

But when I go to lie in sanctuary's colourful meadows
 I notice the cornflowers have grown wild; they dance.
 I think to myself, *We must move closer to the sea.*
 The futility of the year
 Might be the inspiration we need.

BRUSHES

Warbling underwater
  Colours swirl.
  Dip-dive, dip-dash
  Dip, dab, dab
  Screech-scratch.
  Tiny bird feet.
Spattering
Smudging, sloshing.
Tin-tin-tincture.
Tinkle-tickle-scrub.
Rush, hurry, scribble.
Rush-rush-hush.
Sweep-scribble-sweep.
The sound of your brushes
Becoming
The rhythm I love.

BLISSFULLY

Watching the flowers.
  Sat-chit-ananda
  They breathe me in.
  Sat-chit-ananda
  I am free.

Sat-chit-ananda
  I tap my drum.
  Sat-chit-ananda
  I tap my roots.
  Sat-chit-ananda
  I bow my stalk.
  Sat-chit-ananda
  I thank you.

RETREAT

Mulch: universal scent of nature
   Regeneration of composted souls.
   We inhale earth's wisdom:
   Bonds that require dedication.

In the evening, we will build a fire
   Throwing bones to appease the shadows.
   As smoke tickles our throats
   Hallucinations call the ghosts of our ancestors.
   They will retreat into the trees
   Carrying the children with them
   Who had a right to a future.
   They speak Assan by the river
   No one can understand them

COPRINOPSIS ATRAMENTARIA

Untouched and unblemished spores
  Gold-topped church bells on the forest floor;
  Charred skirts seeping with ink
  That will write messages on our skin,

Dulcity from the grand fins of microscopic instruments
  French horn oozing with an oily bass.
  Organs unseen above tubules and botuli.
  They group in formidable megacities, or as gentle elders.

In the wind, the mycelial maestros
  Compress, contract and eject a breath-like embolism.
  In a fleeting concerto, words escape meaning
  as the light lines direct the gifted composer.

The fallen ones, strewn callously across the path,
  Beyond cut piano strings in a mass grave,
  They too will be nutrients for the grateful.
  They will feed mysterious compositions
  When ancestors and descendants reclaim
  A cycle of consumption, that finally benefits all.

MINSTRELS AND MINERALS

Sugar brought to the shore to share a plan
   Now algae and fungus are partners, arm in arm
   Wrapped around each other to survive.
   And, after many years of coexistence,
   Hyphae siege through rocks.
   They are mystic miners riding the contours
   Bursting through channels of their own making,

Natural cables carrying the ethereal
   Shaping our world and hiding secrets, the dawn music;
   The fungus among us; the algae blooms.

HUNTED

Owls howl and I suspect foul play.
  Hunters, blood and gunshots
  Tear through the break of day.
  A flock beats forth with a thousand wings
  Surging through the skies in defiant protest.
  Escaping guns' blasts; their ringing echoes.

As animal skin is peeled back from once-proud bones,
  The fox's spirit watches in vengeful silence
  Bearing its own paring knife in clenched teeth.
  Waiting for an opportunity to slice the skin,
  Make her own mark
  Nature is on her side.

RELIEF

The travellers hat is pinned
  By an arrow fired in passion.
  Hanging from the tree is a tethered crook.

Corpus Christi
  Tarred and feathered.
  A raven feeding
  On his scarecrow toes.

Brass relief
  By an unknown artist.
  The devil in his mind.

WINTER STUDY

Ancestors seen through the window of a winter study
    Not far from the coast.
    Birch, pine, ash and oak rise
    To teach our kind the names of our lungs.

Poems seep through typewriter ribbon like sand eels.
    In remembrance of pleasant days spent outdoors.
    Although nature's broad shoulders
    Cannot bear a selfish species alone.
    We can breathe and feed together.

MORNING FROST

Outside, the bracing air hastens our pace.
  But the warmly-wrapped
  Will pause rosily at frozen buds –
  And sugar-coated blades
  Welcoming the morning frost.

SAPLING

Joy is found seeping from the branches;
   In spirals of cedarwood inhaled.

We unwrap our natural world from the inside;
   Its guises and fond turpentine strip the soul.
   I embrace the mind's dream.

In the wake of yesterday's mortal medicine, we ingest ashes.
   The flames grow indigo.

FREEDOM

Bell jars and musty papers lined desks and shelves,
  Their theses and experiments having dishevelled the hair of
  many
  Chemists, cartographers, cardiologists.

The first of these specialists offered a misjudged reaction.
  The second, misplaced boundaries.
  The third dissected the magic of a human heart:

Beating as you listen now

Ba-dum: Ba-dum
  Ba-dum: Ba-dum

The sound of freedom.

ARDHANARISHVARA

Ardhanarishvara
  The mask has dropped.
  The search has found an end.
  I am content with both sides
  Of a jackal's face
  Pitted only by laughter lines.
  I celebrate diversity
  Silver hands scattered with roses and salt.
  From the river; sandalwood and camber.
  We dance in a festival of light.
  We dance in a festival of life.

NURSERY

Tactile fingers trace
   Over knots and whirls.
   Gnarly, twisted branches curl around knurls.
   Hurl rings that unfurl into
   Bark mottled under moss:
   We learn from our elders
   Now encased by oak.

ALSO BY DANIEL MCCOSH

Escaping
Dream Factory
Da Capo
Aspire

Available from: http://escaping.mccosh.de/

ABOUT THE AUTHOR

Daniel McCosh is a poet and translator based in Fürth, Germany, originally from the UK. He writes poetry from the soul in English and German and is passionate about conserving our natural heritage, finding joy in unexpected places and spreading the magic of poetry in its many forms.